WORD PERFECT
SPELLING

BOOK THREE

Ronald Ridout

Ginn is an imprint of Pearson Education Limited, a company incorporated in England and Wales, having its registered office at Edinburgh Gate, Harlow, Essex, Cm20 2JE, Registered company number: 872828

www.ginn.co.uk

Text © Ronald Ridout, 1957

First published 1957
Revised edition 2008
Reprinted in 2010
12 11 10
10 9 8 7 6 5 4

British Library Cataloguing in Publication Data is available from the British Library on request.

ISBN 978 0 435996 66 6

Typeset an illustrated by Planman Technologies India Pvt. Ltd
Original illustrations © Pearson Education Ltd, 2008
Cover design by Tony Richardson
Cover illustration © Pearson Education Ltd, 2008
Printed by Multivista Global Limited

Every effort has been made to contact copyright holders of material reproduced in this book. Any omissions will be rectified in subsequent printings if notice is given to the publishers.

PREFACE

THE Introductory and eight main books of Word Perfect Spelling provide a systematic course in spelling and vocabulary for primary and secondary schools. Although the books aim firstly at teaching correct spelling, at the same time they help the pupil to gain a complete knowledge of the fundamental vocabulary needed throughout life.

Placing words in certin patterns enables them to be recalled with a greater ease, both in the short and long term. In addition, it allows one key word to unlock many more. This is the main method used in the series, although other styles have been used for specific exercises.

The course, however, does not end with the listing of words: it only begins there. The words have to be linked with the child's interests and brought to life by challenging activities. These activities are in themselves valuable aids to the teaching of English, but they have a vital function in improving spelling.

In Book Three the first few pages are used to revise many of the patterns met in Book Two. Moreover, some of the later exercises also are used for revision, so that a sense of continuity is secured throughout the course. In all, some 560 words from earlier books are revised.

Although in Book Three the formation of correct habits is still the main foundation of learning to spell, an increasing attempt is made to explain the principles involved. As a consequence, simple rules are formulated on pages 6, 10, 12, 20, 21 and 31.

New patterns are introduced at a steady rate, and some 949 new words are met, many of which are practised more than once. It is considered more than ever important to ensure that the meaning of new words is thoroughly grasped, and in the exercises greater emphasis is now placed on this aspect of the work. A test for meaning is given at regular intervals on pages 15, 29 and 44.

brick	bless	bound	child
bust	block	club	damp
tie	grand	hook	why
belt	heel	card	while

brick	bless	bound	child
bust	block	club	damp
tie	grand	hook	why
belt	heel	card	while

1 Instead of *br* in <u>brick</u> write: *tr, th, st, cl, fl.*

2 Instead of *b* in <u>bust</u> write: *d, j, m, r, tr, cr.*

3 Instead of *t* in <u>tie</u> write: *l, p, d.*

4 Instead of *b* in <u>belt</u> write: *f, m, sm, sp.*

5 Instead of *bl* in <u>bless</u> write: *m, l, dr, pr, cr.*

6 Instead of *bl* in <u>block</u> write: *d, m, cl, fl, sh, fr, st, kn.*

7 Instead of *gr* in <u>grand</u> write: *b, h, l, s, st, husb.*

8 Instead of *h* in <u>heel</u> write: *f, p, st, wh, kn.*

9 Instead of *b* in <u>bound</u> write: *f, h, m, p, r, s, w, gr, ar.*

10 Instead of *cl* in <u>club</u> write: *r, t, h, c, gr, sn, shr, scr.*

11 Instead of *h* in <u>hook</u> write: *b, c, l, r, t, sh, br, cr.*

12 Instead of *c* in <u>card</u> write: *y, h, l, cow, must, wiz, forw, cust.*

13 Instead of *ch* in <u>child</u> write: *m, w.*

14 Instead of *d* in <u>damp</u> write: *c, l, st, cr, tr, cl, sw.*

15 Instead of *wh* in <u>why</u> write: *m, fl, fr, cr, tr, dr, sh, sl.*

16 Instead of *wh* in <u>while</u> write: *f, m, p, t, st, sm, fert.*

17 Instead of *k* in <u>hook</u> write: *d, f, p, t, ter.*

18 Instead of *st* in <u>bust</u> write: *zz, mp, nch, ng, lb, cket.*

cake	leaf	frog	beach
spoon	twig	weed	spade
plate	branch	water	swimmer
bread	bird	tadpole	children
desk	dress	apples	sheets
chalk	frock	soap	chair
pencils	skirt	eggs	brushes
teacher	gloves	butter	slippers
train	letters	eye	Tuesday
porter	words	ear	Wednesday
driver	paper	arm	Thursday
tickets	sentences	mouth	Friday

These are words that you have met before. Can you still spell them? Write down the four most likely to be:

1 at the seaside
2 in a school
3 at the grocer's
4 on the tea-table
5 on a tree
6 in a pond
7 in a book
8 in a wardrobe
9 in a bedroom
10 on a calendar
11 at a station
12 belonging to a body

Once upon a time there was a young boy who was never tidy. He left his books on the chairs and his muddy shoes on the table. He put his fingers in the pudding and then wiped them on his shirt. He upset paint on his best clothes, and he dropped tooth-paste on the bathroom floor. He hardly ever brushed his hair. He was so untidy that we called him Tidy Tom as a joke.

past	swing	wiped	muddy
paste	finger	tidy	dropped
fast	once	untidy	pudding
fasten	clothes	hardly	young

Write out ten words in the box that can be built from the letters in this sentence:

OUR DONALD WAS FRYING THE POTATOES.

slight	cool	done	sprang
fright	roof	none	sang
sight	broom	some	slang
might	stood	gone	rang
scrap	lift	again	died
strap	swift	against	cried
slack	silk	obtain	dried
swank	thinner	grain	carried
shabby	trigger	faint	married

Can you arrange the first list in alphabetical order? **Fright** comes before **might**, because **f** comes before **m** in the alphabet. But if two words begin with the same letter, you must look at the second letters. Thus **sight** comes before **slight**, because **i** comes before **l**. In alphabetical order the same list is: **fright, might, sight, slight**.

Now arrange the other lists in alphabetical order, and number them 1 to 7.

8 Arrange this list in alphabetical order:
 tried, flight, foolish, something, finish, strain

ABCDEFGHIJKLMNOPQRSTUVWXYZ

1	three, two, one	20	two, ten, twenty
2	one, two, three	21	one, ten, twenty-one
3	two, one, three	22	twenty-two, two, eleven
4	three, four, five	28	twenty, twenty-eight, two
5	five, six, seven		
6	four, five, six	30	ten, twenty, thirty
7	six, seven, eight	40	forty, thirty, twenty
8	eight, seven, six	50	forty, fifty, sixty
9	seven, eight, nine	60	sixty, forty, twenty
10	nine, ten, eleven	70	thirty, fifty, seventy
11	seven, nine, eleven	80	sixty, seventy, eighty
12	eight, ten, twelve	90	ninety, one hundred, eighty
13	thirteen, eleven, nine	100	eighty, one hundred, ninety
14	fourteen, ten, six	106	ten, six, one hundred and six
15	five, ten, fifteen		
16	four, sixteen, eight	346	three hundred and forty-six, one
17	seven, seventeen, eleven		
18	seventeen, eighteen, nineteen	1000	one thousand, two thousand
19	eighteen, nineteen, twenty		

(a) Write down the figures and choose the right words to put after them. Begin like this: **1** one   **2** two

(b) Write in words all the even numbers (2, 4, 6, 8, etc.) up to twenty.

(c) Write in words all the odd numbers (1, 3, 5, 7, etc.) up to nineteen.

player	smoker	writer	gardener
owner	grocer	skater	footballer
farmer	driver	draper	hairdresser
butcher	miner	knitter	fishmonger

In each sentence put in the right word from the box.

1 A man who digs coal is called a _____.

2 A man who sells fish is called a _____.

3 A _____ is someone who plays football.

4 A _____ is a man who sells meat.

5 The _____ cut my hair yesterday.

6 The _____ of a cat is the person to whom it belongs.

7 The _____ of this letter is the person who sent it to me.

8 A person who runs a farm is called a _____.

9 Anyone who works in a garden is called a _____.

10 Anyone who takes part in a game is called a _____.

11 The man who drives the bus is called the _____.

12 A _____ is someone who knits.

13 The _____ sold me a pair of sheets and a towel.

14 A man who smokes cigarettes is called a _____.

15 The _____ sold me some bread, eggs and cheese.

16 The _____ glided swiftly across the ice.

Betty bought a bit of butter,
But said, 'My bit of butter's bitter.
If I put it in my batter.
It will make my batter bitter.
Better buy some fresher butter.'
Betty's mother said she'd let her,
So she bought some better butter
And it made her batter better.

better	buy	say	stop
bitter	bought	said	stopped
butter	ought	paid	stopping
batter	thought	afraid	stopper

Stopper comes from the shorter word **stop**.

Write the shorter words that these come from:

1 rubber   3 shopper   5 planning   7 bragging
2 clapped   4 runner   6 skater   8 writing

Complete these tables:

9 thin thinner thinnest   15 flap flapping flapped
10 slim — slimmest   16 drag dragging —
11 — — biggest   17 — fitting —
12 — hotter —   18 slip — —
13 — worse worst   19 bring — brought
14 good — best   20 — saying —

bus	buses	match	matches
dress	dresses	patch	patches
box	boxes	watch	watches
ditch	ditches	glove	gloves
brush	brushes	stove	stoves
branch	branches	month	months

A singular noun means one only. A plural noun means more than one. To make a singular noun plural, we usually add just -s. But if the noun ends in a hissing letter like s, ch, sh or x, we have to add -es.

1 Write out the three plural nouns from the box that have had just -s added to them.

2 Write out the nine plural nouns that have had -es added to them.

Write down the singular nouns from which each of these has been made:

3 branches 5 months 7 brushes 9 dishes
4 watches 6 gloves 8 glasses 10 churches

Write down the plural of these nouns:

11 match 13 bus 15 class 17 stove
12 patch 14 box 16 thrush 18 peach

first

second

third

firsh   toffees

second   sugar

third   coal

fourth   carrots

fifth   apples

sixth   bottles

seventh   chocolates

eighth   potatoes

eighth

seventh

sixth

fourth   fifth

Draw the bags and write on each to say what is inside. Then write eight sentences, beginning like this:

    1 The first bag is full of chocolates.

    2 The second bag is full of ....

Complete these:

    9 one shoe but two shoes

10 one ____ but two dresses

11 one ____ but two buses

12 one fox but two ____

13 one apple but six ____

14 one ____ but four matches

15 one chocolate but six ____

16 one ____ but two bottles

17 one church but two ____

18 one bush but nine ____ ,

19 one ____ but two doves

20 one catch but eight ____

aunt	ounce	instant	prince
uncle	inch	infant	princess
prison	bench	order	poem
apron	branch	border	poet

The five vowels are: a, e, i, o, u. All the other letters of the alphabet are consonants.

We use **a** before a word that begins with a consonant, but we must use **an** before a word beginning with a vowel. Thus we say a lesson, but an inch. We say an odd uncle, but a broken branch.

1   Write out all the consonants.

2–17   Write out the words from the box, putting **a** or **an** in front of each. Number them 2–17.

Write out these, putting **a** or **an** in each gap:

18 ____ ounce of pepper

19 in ____ instant

20 ____ long lesson

21 ____ rich prince

22 ____ empty bench

23 ____ short poem

24 ____ even border

25 ____ old scarf

26 ____ prince and ____ princess

27 ____ aunt in ____ apron

28 ____ oven in the kitchen

29 in ____ few minutes

30 ____ oil-can in his hand

31 as ____ gift

32 ____ apple a day

33 ____ oak tree and ____ elm

Diana Brown likes drawing. In the summer she sits on the lawn and draws. One day she drew a man going to work. Then she drew the man falling into the river. Next, she drew another man diving into the

river after him. Last of all, she drew a large crowd. Everyone was clapping the diver because he had saved the other man from drowning.

town	word	law	crowd
brown	worm	claw	worth
crown	work	straw	drawing
drown	world	lawn	worker

1 Instead of *s* in <u>s</u>aw write: *l, p, r, j, cl, dr, str, outl.*

2 Instead of *d* in wor<u>d</u> write: *m, k, th, ld, se, st, ship.*

3 Instead of *l* in <u>l</u>awn write: *d, s, y, dr, sp.*

4 Instead of *t* in <u>t</u>own write: *d, br, cr, cl, dr, fr, gr.*

soft	shave	steam	shape
often	slave	dream	cheat
soften	shade	scream	squeak
softly	grape	steal	after

1 From the box below choose the six words that have the same short *o* vowel sound as you can hear in <u>soft</u>.

both	soften	toffees	bottle	Joyce	lower
often	loaf	shoes	pound	John	lorries

2 From this box choose the six words that have the same long *a* vowel sound as you can hear in <u>shape</u>.

grape	steam	shade	waste	fatter	April
cheat	shave	scream	fasten	draper	March

Arrange these lists in alphabetical order. If in doubt, turn back to page 6.

3 Jane	4 Richard	5 Jean	6 Charles
Grace	Betty	John	Andrew
Kate	Ronald	Jill	Thomas
George	Simon	James	Clare
David	Jessica	Judy	Cecil

1 `[ ][a][s][ ][ ]` You can stick paper with this. (page 5)

2 `[ ][ ][h][ ]` The number that comes after seven. (7)

3 `[ ][ ][a][n][ ][ ][ ][ ]` The plural of branch. (10)

4 `[ ][ ][ ][ ][e][n]` To make soft. (14)

5 `[ ][ ][t][ ][ ]` Many times. (14)

6 `[ ][ ][ ][ ][e][r]` Anyone who works is called this. (13)

7 `[ ][ ][g][ ][ ]` This is used to make food sweet. (11)

8 `[ ][ ][ ][h]` There are twelve of these in a foot. (12)

9 `[ ][ ][ ][g]` The opposite of old. (5)

10 `[ ][ ][ ][ ][y][t][ ][ ]` Twice eleven make this number. (7)

11 `[ ][ ][ ][a][ ]` To do something unfairly. (14)

12 `[ ][ ][ ][ ][e][r]` A man who sells meat. (8)

13 `[ ][ ][t][ ][b][ ][ ][ ][ ][ ]` A person who plays football. (8)

14 `[ ][b][ ][ ][ ][ ]` To get. (6)

15 `[ ][ ][o][o][ ][ ]` A kind of brush. (6)

16 `[ ][ ][ ][p][ ][ ]` A baby frog. (4)

17 `[ ][ ][ ][ ][ ][ ][ ]` Fat to spread on bread. (9)

18 `[ ][ ][ ][ ][ ][ ][ ]` The plural of ditch. (10)

19 `[ ][ ][ ][ ][ ][ ][ ][ ][ ]` A man who sells fish. (8)

20 `[ ][ ][ ][ ][ ][ ]` Wine is made from this fruit. (14)

21 `[ ][ ][ ][ ][ ][ ]` The singular of dresses. (10)

22 `[ ][ ][ ][ ][ ][ ][ ][ ]` The day after Tuesday. (4)

23 `[ ][ ][ ][ ][ ][ ][ ]` A child under the age of seven. (12)

Let's make sure

(1)

lead	harm	water	joke
beads	march	bathe	spoke
beach	part	seaside	close
teacher	party	diver	wrote

(2)

lift	dead	getting	band
swift	bread	batting	blank
mist	ahead	better	crab
print	instead	flattest	slack

(3)

eight	sugar	prison	father
twelve	chocolates	lesson	brother
eighty	grocer	apron	baby
hundred	butcher	lemon	infant

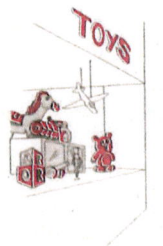 

Mrs Brown walked down the road to do her shopping. She bought some bread from the baker and some meat from the butcher. Then she stepped across the street to the toyshop. There she bought a beach ball for Diana and a little spade for the baby.

January	May	September
February	June	October
March	July	November
April	August	December

1 Write the last month in the year.

2 Write the month that it is now.

3 Write the month that it was last month.

4 Suppose the year went backwards. Write the months in the order they would then come.

5 Write the month in which your birthday comes.

6 Write the months in alphabetical order. (March comes before May, and July comes before June.)

Write these sentences, putting in the right months:

7 The first month of the year is ____.

8 ____ is the last month of the year.

9 After February comes ____.

10 ____ comes after July.

11 ____ comes between January and March.

12 The months between July and October are ____ and ____.

13 ____, ____ and ____ come between February and June.

14 ____, ____, ____ and ____ all end in -er.

Michael Short is just ten years old. He likes helping in the garden. His father has put him in charge of one of the flower-beds. There are forty sunflowers in this bed. They are very large and tall. They tower right up above Michael. There has not been a shower for a long time. So today Michael is busy watering his flowers.

sort	large	power	report
sport	barge	flower	shower
short	charge	tower	busy
forty	great	towel	sunflower

1 Instead of *s* in <u>sort</u> write: *f, p, sh, rep, imp, exp, comf, transp*.

2 Instead of *er* in <u>tower</u> write: *el, n, ered*.

3 Write the first list in alphabetical order.

4 Write the words from the box that are the opposites of these: tiny, tall, idle, work, retreat.

5 Write these words in alphabetical order:

   shower   sunflower   port   power   sport   skirt

cheese   dozen   bottle   currants

kilo   packet   lemonade   sandwiches

gram   oranges   pepper   chocolates

bread   loaf   biscuit   potatoes

a packet of biscuits	a dozen oranges
a bottle of lemonade	a box of chocolates
a packet of sandwiches	a sack of potatoes
a loaf of bread	$\frac{1}{2}$ kilo of currants
a kilo of cheese	$\frac{1}{2}$ kilo of butter
100 grams of sweets	25 grams of pepper

Draw the pictures and put the right description under each one.

stick	sticking	tug	tugging
creep	creeping	drag	dragging
crawl	crawling	skid	skidding
		chop	chopping
write	writing	knit	knitting
choose	choosing	stir	stirring
dance	dancing	strip	stripping

Here are the rules about adding -ing:

(a) To most words you can just add -ing.

(b) But to words ending in *e* you must drop the *e* and then add -ing. (Except words like see, be, tie.)

(c) To words that end with a single consonant before which comes a single vowel you must double the consonant and then add -ing.

From what word has each of these been formed?

1 dancing	3 knitting	5 stopping	7 smoking
2 crawling	4 racing	6 writing	8 swimming

9 Which rule do these follow? Make three equal groups and mark them (a), (b), (c).

stare – staring	pray – praying	please – pleasing
bring – bringing	shop – shopping	knot – knotting
shine – shining	fetch – fetching	whir – whirring

daisy	cities	empty	married
daisies	lilies	emptied	hurries
worry	cherries	carry	pities
worries	parties	carries	tidied

To make the plural of a noun that ends in *y* and has a consonant before the *y*, you must change the *y* into *i* and then add **-es**. Thus we have: army—armies, story—stories.

Write the singular of the following nouns:

1 daisies   3 armies   5 lilies   7 stories   9 ladies
2 worries   4 cherries   6 parties   8 berries   10 babies

Write the plural of these nouns:

11 lily   13 story   15 fairy   17 spy   19 worry
12 party   14 army   16 copy   18 sky   20 baby

In the same way, if a verb ends in *y* with a consonant before the *y*, you must change the *y* into *i* before adding **-es** or **-ed**. Thus we have: hurry—hurries—hurried, reply—replies—replied

Add *-es* and *-ed* to these verbs. Begin like this:

21 bury—buries—buried

21 bury   23 carry   25 try   27 reply   29 marry
22 tidy   24 hurry   26 dry   28 pity   30 empty

chief	happy	bumble	cloth
thief	happen	grumble	clothes
field	rattle	simple	bath
piece	kettle	marble	bathe

Write a word from the list that rhymes with:

1 battle   **2** brief   **3** shield   **4** pimple   **5** niece

Write from the box the word meaning the opposite of:

6 unhappy   **7** proud   **8** difficult   **9** whole

10 Write out the six words that end in **-le**.

Grumbling is made from the shorter word **grumble**. Write the shorter words that these are made from:

11 tumbling   **12** rattling   **13** grumbled   **14** rumbling

15 Write the eight words from the box that can be built from these letters: A B C D E F H I L M P R S T U.

Arrange each list below in alphabetical order:

16 Ruth	**17** Robert	**18** cattle	**19** Jones
Tony	Albert	battle	Thomas
Roger	Arthur	belief	Taylor
Mary	Henry	chief	Jennings
Molly	Harry	field	Price

I – N spells in.
I was in my kitchen
Doing a little stitching.
Old Father Nimble
Came and took my thimble.
I fetched a great big stone
And knocked him on the funny bone.
O – U – T spells out.

fetch	nimble	health	knock
scratch	thimble	healthy	death
kitchen	bundle	wealth	funny
stitching	handle	wealthy	great

Write the words from the box that rhyme with:

1 candle   2 shock   3 sunny   4 thimble   5 catch

6 Instead of *f* in <u>fetch</u> write: *str, sk.*
7 Instead of *st* in <u>stitch</u> write: *w, d, p, sw, tw.*
8 Instead of *scr* in <u>scratch</u> write: *c, m, p, sn, th.*
9 Instead of *b* in <u>bone</u> write: *st, ph, al, thr.*
10 Instead of *th* in <u>death</u> write: *d, f, lt, dly.*
11 Instead of *tch* in <u>fetch</u> write: *ll, lt, nee, nder, rry.*

Make new words by adding *y* to these:

12 dust   14 wealth   16 luck   18 cloud
13 rust   15 health   17 pluck   19 frost

someone	anyone	nowhere	towards
something	anything	nothing	afterwards
sometime	anybody	nobody	forward
somewhere	anywhere	everywhere	together

No and thing make nothing. Can you do these?

1 Be and come make ____.

2 Black and board make ____.

3 After and noon make ____.

4 Butter and fly make ____.

5 Birth and day make ____.

6 Every and one make ____.

7 How and ever make ____.

8 Rain and bow make ____.

9 But and ton make ____.

10 Less and on make ____.

11 Under and stand make ____.

12 For and ward make ____.

13 Re and ward make ____.

14 Break and fast make ____.

15 Be and fore make ____.

16 Be and lieve make ____.

Pair each word with its opposite. Begin like this:

17 something—nothing

18 nowhere

17 something	poor	23 afterwards	nobody
18 nowhere	heavy	24 black	saving
19 light	nothing	25 great	before
20 hating	backward	26 spending	white
21 wealthy	loving	27 often	little
22 forward ·	somewhere	28 somebody	never

This is the key of a country.
In that country there is a county.
In that county there is a village.
In that village there is a square.
In that square there is a cottage.
In that cottage there is a room.
In that room there is a table.
On that table there is a basket,
And in that basket there are some flowers.

village	town	county	table
cottage	flower	country	unable
cabbage	dare	mountain	basket
garage	square	fountain	ticket

1 Write the jingle backwards, beginning like this:

      The flowers were in the basket.

      The basket was on

2 Instead of *d* in dare write: *c, f, r, sp, st, sq, sh, sc, aw, bew.*

3 Instead of *t* in ticket write: *w, cr.*

4 Instead of *t* in table write: *st. c, f, un, cap.*

5 Instead of *fl* in flower write: *p, t, sh.*

Write the plural of these nouns:

6 county   7 country   8 ferry   9 square   10 basket

aches	our	never	soon
ape	sour	every	steer
shape	aloud	shed	idea
busy	enough	roar	area

1		2		3		4
			5	6 U		
			7	P		
8				9		

Draw your own puzzle. Then use some of the words from the box to solve it. Here are the clues:

Across

1 To guide.

3 Pains that go on and on.

5 Belonging to us.

7 Tail-less animal that can walk on two feet.

8 The opposite of always.

9 Not in a whisper.

Down

1 In a short time.

2 A loud deep sound.

3 Amount of surface.

4 A building used to store things.

6 The opposite of down.

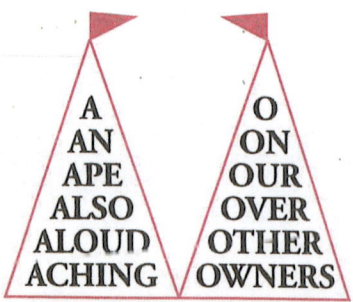

```
A           O
AN          ON
APE         OUR
ALSO        OVER
ALOUD       OTHER
ACHING      OWNERS
```

These are word tents. Each word has to have one more letter than the one above it. Make another tent, beginning with A. Then make one with the words beginning with I.

If you want to keep healthy
you must make sure
that your teeth are clean.
It is a good plan
to brush them every night
before going to bed.
In the picture you can see
John in the bathroom.
He has a tube of tooth-paste.
He is just going to put some
on his tooth-brush.
What kind of tooth-paste
do you use for your teeth?

tub	tube	rude	pure
cub	cube	tune	sure
cur	cure	fuse	picture
us	use	refuse	excuse

Notice that when you add a silent *e* to <u>tub</u>, the short vowel sound *u* becomes a long vowel sound. Make new words by adding a silent *e* to:

1 slid   **2** cub   **3** slop   **4** spin   **5** cur   **6** scrap

<u>Curing</u> comes from <u>cure</u>. What do these come from?

7 using   **8** refusing   **9** sliding   **10** excusing   **11** tuning

high	knee	lamb	quite
light	kneel	comp	alone
brought	knock	climb	above
thought	knot	thumb	starve

Notice the silent letters. In the first list *gh* is silent. In the second it is *k*. In the third it is *b*, and in the last it is *e*.

Arrange these words in four lists in the same way:

knit	strike	climbing	nought
thought	scrape	knitting	thumbs
axe	knelt	kneeling	brought
crumb	fought	combing	flame

Pair each numbered word with its opposite.

1	high	many	9 bought	wrong
2	above	dull	10 right	rude
3	few	empty	11 light	ill
4	bright	hard	12 valive	sold
5	full	low	13 liked	highest
6	asleep	below	14 lowest	dead
7	easy	took away	15 polite	hated
8	brought	awake	16 healthy	heavy

1 ☐☐☐ **a g e** Place to keep a car. (page 25)

2 ☐☐☐☐ **i e s** Plural of daisy. (21)

3 ☐☐ **e e** ☐ To go down on your knees. (28)

4 ☐☐☐ **t y** To take everything out. (21)

5 ☐☐☐☐☐ The opposite of polite. (27)

6 ☐☐☐☐ **t h** ☐ Means the same as rich. (23)

7 ☐ **c h** ☐☐ Pains that go on and on. (26)

8 ☐☐☐☐☐ **y** The first month of the year. (17)

9 ☐ **o w** ☐☐ You can dry your hands on this. (18)

10 ☐☐☐☐ **y** You are this when you have a lot to do. (18)

11 ☐☐ **e a** ☐ This comes from boiling water. (14)

12 ☐☐ **t** ☐☐ To go and get. (23)

13 ☐☐☐☐☐ You can make dresses from this material. (22)

14 ☐☐☐☐☐☐☐ The plural of orange. (19)

15 ☐☐☐☐☐. To pick out. (20)

16 ☐☐☐☐☐ The singular of worries. (21)

17 ☐☐☐☐☐☐ A person who knits. (8)

18 ☐☐☐☐☐ Means the same as a part. (22)

19 ☐☐☐☐☐☐ You take hold of this. (23)

20 ☐☐☐☐☐ You carry your shopping in this. (25)

21 ☐☐☐☐☐☐ The opposite of everything. (24)

22 ☐☐☐☐☐ To have nothing to eat. (28)

23 ☐☐☐☐☐ This is a person who steals. (22)

Let's make sure

(4)

chew	price	began	float
flew	twice	begun	coast
crew	clay	being	soak
threw	pray	become	roar

(5)

soil	vain	better	rage
spoil	rail	cutter	trade
coin	laid	knitter	grave
voice	raise	spanner	waste

(6)

bread	enter	dance	work
spread	tender	dancing	since
instead	spider	chance	change
ready	poker	glance	changing

Jane likes helping her mother. She always lays the table for tea. Afterwards she washes up and dries the dishes. On Saturday mornings she polishes the floor, and then goes shopping.

half	halves	wife	wives
shelf	shelves	knife	knives
loaf	loaves	thief	thieves
leaf	leaves	himself	themselves

When a noun ends in *f*, you often have to change the *f* into *v* and then add -**es** to make the plural.

With a word ending in -**fe**, you must change the *f* into *v* and add only -**s**, because the *e* is already there.

Write the singular of these nouns:

1 leaves   3 halves   5 thieves   7 wolves

2 wives   4 calves   6 scarves   8 lives

Write the plural of these nouns:

9 shelf   11 calf   13 knife   15 life   17 himself

10 thief   12 wife   14 wolf   16 elf   18 scarf

Arrange each list in alphabetical order:

19 shelves	20 elves	21 knots	22 excuses
loaves	flowers	sights	cubes
thieves	thumbs	keys	combs
leaves	knees	thrushes	tubes
wives	calves	teeth	themselves
halves	crumbs	stitches	towers
knives	churches	showers	chocolates

On Easter Monday John had breakfast early, so that he could visit the zoo. It was not a long journey, and he was soon there. He paid his money and went inside. He looked at the lions, tigers and bears first. Then he visited the cages where the monkeys lived. There he met a friend. No, it was not a monkey! It was Peter from the next street. After they had seen all the monkeys, they had a ride together on an elephant.

lion	wolf	money	Easter
tiger	deer	monkey	early
bear	camel	journey	friend
zebra	visit	elephant	breakfast

Write the singular of:

1 camels   3 wolves   5 monkeys   7 tigers
2 friends   4 journeys 6 calves   8 watches

Make new words by adding these endings to visit:

9 -s   10 -ed   11 -ing   12 -or   13 -ors

Write the words from the box that rhyme with:

14 honey   15 steer   16 rare   17 yearly   18 mend

bus	aeroplane	bicycle	liner
car	seaplane	tricycle	yacht
lorry	helicopter	motorcycle	lifeboat
tractor	airliner	scooter	submarine

Write these, putting in the words from the box:

1 A _____ has pedals and two wheels.

2 A _____ has pedals and three wheels.

3 A _____ is a bicycle driven by a motor.

4 A child drives a _____ by pushing on the ground with one foot. It is also a name for a light motorcycle.

5 A large passenger boat is called a _____.

6 Goods are taken by road in a _____.

7 A _____ is like a big car that carries many people.

8 Four or five people can travel by road in a _____.

9 An _____ is driven by propellers or jets and can land only on the ground.

10 A _____, however, can land on water.

11 A _____ can land almost straight down.

12 A sailing boat used for racing is called a _____.

13 An _____ is an aeroplane that carries many passengers.

14 A _____ is used for pulling things over rough ground.

15 A ship that sails under water is called a _____.

16 A _____ is used for making rescues at sea.

ragged	rascal	clever	pickled
rugged	stripe	river	tickled
pepper	piper	polite	paddled
rubber	wiper	invite	cuddled

Peter Piper picked a peck of pickled pepper;
A peck of pickled pepper Peter Piper picked.
If Peter Piper picked a peck of pickled pepper,
Where is the peck of pickled pepper Peter Piper picked?

Round and round the rugged rock
The ragged rascal ran.
Say how many R's in that
And you're a clever man.

odd	build	listen	buy
usual	built	earth	laugh
music	building	plenty	people
huge	sign	present	view

This is an extra list. You will often need these odd words; so make sure you can spell them.

1 Write the eight words that can be built from the letters of this sentence:

WAS ROBIN HOOD BOLD ENOUGH TO WIN?

2 Write in alphabetical order the eight that are left.

There was an old man who said, "Well!
Will nobody answer this bell?
I have pulled day and night
Till my hair has turned white,
But nobody answers the bell!"

loose	wear	quick	answer
goose	bear	quickly	freeze
geese	tear	quiet	weary
cheese	pear	quietly	question

Write the adjectives from which these adverbs come:

1 quickly   3 loosely   5 rudely   7 selfishly

2 quietly   4 politely   6 silently   8 wrongly

Choose one of the adverbs above to fill each gap:

9 John ran ____ and soon caught the goose.

10 Susan answered the question quite ____ when she said that two and two make five.

11 The picture was hanging so ____ that it fell down as soon as I touched it.

12 Christopher very ____ left no pudding for his sister.

13 With a soft voice you can speak ____ but never ____.

14 The opposite of speaking ____ is speaking ____.

shirt	penny	won	month
skirt	pennies	wonder	monk
birth	pence	wonderful	squirt
third	fence	Monday	birthday

JANUARY

Sunday		6	13	20	27
Monday		7	14	21	28
Tuesday	1	8	15	22	29
Wednesday	2	9	16	23	30
Thursday	3	10	17	24	31
Friday	4	11	18	25	
Saturday	5	12	19	26	

1 Margaret: 2nd January
2 Philip: 5th January
3 Paul: 9th January
4 Diana: 12th January
5 Ian: 16th January
6 Elizabeth: 19th January
7 Sheila: 23rd January
8 Norman: 26th January
9 Alan: 31st January

On the right above are the dates of the birthdays of nine children. On what days will their birthdays be? Begin your answers like this: **1** *Margaret's birthday will be on a Wednesday.*

Arrange each of these lists in alphabetical order:

10 Christine	**11** Michael	**12** Elizabeth	**13** Morris
Jennifer	Margaret	Ernest	Austin
Colin	Douglas	Donald	Hillman
John	David	Derek	Standard
Judith	Arthur	Diana	Singer
Charles	Andrew	Ethel	Ford

Here is the weather forecast. Today it will be warm and sunny in Wales and the south of England. In the north of England there will be some showers late in the day. In

Scotland it will be foggy at first, and in the afternoon there may be thunder-storms. Tomorrow's outlook is less good. It will be dull and cloudy over the whole of the British Isles, and rain is likely to spread from the west.

yesterday	thunder	foggy	England
tomorrow	lighting	sunny	Scotland
weather	sunshine	storm	Wales
forecast	dull	gale	British Isles

1 Instead of *w* in <u>weather</u> write: *f, l, h.*
2 In front of <u>under</u> write: *th, bl, pl.*
3 Instead of *ll* in <u>dull</u> write: *st, sk, ck, sty, ster.*
4 Instead of *st* in <u>frost</u> write: *ck, g, m, nt, sty, wn.*
5 Instead of *Eng* in <u>England</u> write: *Scot, Ire, is, main, Hol.*
6 Instead of *m* in <u>storm</u> write: *e, k, my, y.*
7 Instead of *g* in <u>gale</u> write: *p, t, s, st, sc, wh.*

reply	hummer	sorry	mother
repeat	stammer	silly	copper
funny	summer	hilly	river
furry	sudden	spilling	penny

Each of these words has two parts. Thus, **summer** is made up of **sum** and **mer**. We call these parts syllables. **Summer** has two syllables.

From each group of syllables below, make up the two words asked for. All the words are in the box.

ny   pen   fun

1 a copper coin
2 another word for amusing

er   riv   moth

3 a woman who has children
4 a very large stream

fur   sor   ry

5 covered with fur
6 feeling regret

peat   ply   re

7 to say again
8 to give an answer

mer   ham   sum

9 tool for knocking in nails
10 the season that follows spring

ly   hil   sil

11 full of hills
12 not sensible

polish	forgive	across	afraid
finish	forget	above	forest
punish	forbid	around	English
furnish	forward	alike	British

Add the missing syllable to each of these, to make one of the words in the box:

1 ____ give	5 pol ____	9 ____ ward	13 fin ____
2 ____ bove	6 Eng ____	10 ____ round	14 ____ fraid
3 ____ est	7 Bri ____	11 pun ____	15 furn ____
4 ____ get	8 ____ bid	12 ____ like	16 ____ cross

Divide these words into two syllables each:

17 cannot	21 upstairs	25 between	29 England
18 before	22 himself	26 carpet	30 Tuesday
19 forget	23 summer	27 unless	31 July
20 across	24 snowdrop	28 invite	32 Betty

Some words have three syllables. Thus, **afternoon** can be divided like this: af – ter – noon. (Notice that every syllable has a vowel in it.)

Divide these words into three syllables each:

33 yesterday	37 November	41 polishing
34 suddenly	38 December	42 punishment
35 understand	39 forgiven	43 forbidden
36 understood	40 forgotten	44 butterfly

baked	tried	nibbled	viewed
enjoyed	stole	gobbled	inspected
munched	fought	captured	reached
wanted	lifted	quartered	heated
divided	upset	pointed	
opened	kept	jumped	

Write out this alphabet, putting in the right words from the box.
The first three have been done to show you how to carry on.

A was an apple pie.

B baked it.

C captured it.

D ___ it.

E ___ it.

F ___ for it.

G ___ it.

H ___ it.

I ___ it.

J ___ for it.

K ___ it.

L ___ it.

M ___ it.

N ___ it.

O ___ it.

P ___ at it.

Q ___ it.

R ___ for it.

S ___ it.

T ___ it.

U ___ it.

V ___ it.

W ___ it.

X Y Z all longed for it.

Andrew was a lucky boy. His parents took him for a holiday in France. They went to London Airport by coach. They saw many aeroplanes taking off and touching down. Soon Andrew was climbing into an airliner. The pilot revved up the engine. The airliner raced down the runway. A moment later they were airborne. Far below them they could see the river, roads and houses growing smaller and smaller.

France	airport	revved	pilot
London	airliner	raced	engine
Andrew	airborne	touching	parents
aeroplane	coach	climbing	holiday

return	lose	excite	prove
remain	loser	exciting	improve
repair	move	enjoy	depart
remark	remove	enjoyable	suddenly

The vowels have been left out. Put them in, and write out the words and their meanings.

1 R _ M _ V _   To take away.
2 R _ M _ _ N   To stay where you are.
3 D – P – R T   To go away.
4 R _ T _ R N   To come back.
5 L _ S _ R   A person who loses.
6 S _ D D _ N L Y   All of a sudden.
7 _ N J _ Y _ B L _   Able to be enjoyed.
8 _ M P R _ V _   To become better.
9 R _ P _ _ R   To make good again.
10 _ X C _ T _ N G   Which stirs up one's feelings.

Can you make these into words ending in **-ing**?

11 excite   14 enjoy   17 remove   20 begin
12 lose   15 repair   18 dig   21 waste
13 improve   16 invite   19 forget   22 glide

Make adjectives by adding **-able** to these verbs:

23 enjoy   24 remark   25 agree   26 obtain   27 suit

Make adverbs by adding **-ly** to these adjectives:

28 sudden   29 quiet   30 fair   31 unfair   32 clever

thirst	dirty	hasty	tiny
thirsty	stormy	icy	nasty
taste	weary	tidy	noisy
tasty	sleepy	rosy	wavy

Make new words by adding *y* to these:

1 rain	4 thirst	7 curl	10 fair
2 dirt	5 health	8 bus	11 read
3 wind	6 wealth	9 part	12 ever

Notice that when you add *y* to a word ending in a silent *e*, like taste, you have to drop the *e* and then add *y*. Now make new words by adding *y* to these:

13 haste	16 shine	19 bone	22 laze
14 ice	17 shade	20 stone	23 craze
15 wave	18 rose	21 noise	24 juice

Pair each adjective with its opposite.

25 tasty	quiet	32 nasty	ugly
26 noisy	full	33 ready	shaky
27 dirty	tasteless	34 steady	nice
28 empty	straight	35 tiny	polite
29 cloudy	clean	36 early	huge
30 heavy	light	37 pretty	late
31 wavy	sunny	38 rude	unready

1 [ ][ ][c][h][ ] Place where you cook. (page 23)

2 [ ][ ][P][h][ ][ ] Largest animal in the world. (32)

3 [ ][ ][e][r] A person who loses. (42)

4 [ ][o][l][ ][ ] The opposite of rude. (34)

5 [ ][ ][ ][ ][o][w] The day after today. (37)

6 [ ][z][ ][ ] Another way of saying twelve. (19)

7 [ ][ ][ ][i][e][s] The plural of penny. (36)

8 [ ][ ][ ][ ][t][y] Needing a drink. (43)

9 [ ][o][o][ ] The opposite of tight. (35)

10 [ ][ ][ ][v][ ] The plural of thief. (31)

11 [ ][ ][m][a][ ][ ][ ] A ship that sails under the water. (33)

12 [ ][ ][w][ ] You give this to a question. (35)

13 [ ][ ][ ][ ] The one before the fourth. (36)

14 [ ][ ][ ][ ][ ] Making a lot of noise. (43)

15 [ ][ ][ ][ ][ ] To come back. (42)

16 [ ][ ][ ][ ][ ][ ] Mother and father. (41)

17 [ ][b][b][ ][ ] Took little bites. (40)

18 [ ][ ][ ][ ][ ] A large wood. (39)

19 [ ][ ][ ][ ][ ] The season that follows spring. (38)

20 [ ][ ][ ][ ] Having plenty to do. (18)

21 [ ][ ][ ][d][s] The opposite of away from. (24)

22 [ ][ ][ ][ ][ ][ ][ ][ ][ ] A person who cuts hair. (8)

23 [ ][ ][ ][ ][ ] Means the same as to end. (39)

Let's make sure

(7)

path	utter	treat	gather
bath	suffer	eaten	steam
rather	rubber	beaten	manner
father	offer	broken	matter

(8)

dinner	brought	wool	battle
ladder	fought	stool	muddle
rabbit	worse	bloom	little
bottom	worst	blood	settle

(9)

charm	cheer	friend	cradle
charge	feeling	people	gentle
farmer	indeed	women	needle
army	weedy	children	tumble

Last year we spent a whole month of our summer holidays in the country. We stayed on Uncle John's farm. I liked riding on the tractor best, but Judy hought that riding the pony was better.

For extra work

(1)

careless	heart	pillow	nurse
careful	hearth	yellow	purse
useful	heaven	shallow	burst
useless	dreadful	hollow	burnt

(2)

person	content	illness	scout
pardon	moment	darkness	guide
serve	defend	shadow	whistle
term	pretend	dying	explore

(3)

anger	cover	chimney	station
angry	silver	cupboard	travel
hunger	shelter	animal	voyage
hungry	murder	history	adventure

(4)

darling	beginning	easy	Christmas
starling	together	easier	Christine
partner	enough	heavy	Christopher
farther	cough	heavier	Christian